# Praise for *John Henry Newman*

"Dr. Marr's book is timely and certain to be well received. The collection of readings from Newman's vast number of works is arranged thematically and is helpful to the reader who is seeking a brief introduction to Newman's thought. It is also suitable for *lectio divina*, a contemplative reading of the texts. Dr. Marr's introduction, with its personal reflections, provides a context that will draw the reader into Newman's life and thought, and helps to explain why Saint John Henry Newman matters today."

— Kenneth L. Parker, Ryan Endowed Chair for
Newman Studies, Duquesne University

"Saint John Henry Newman is considered one of the most prolific and accomplished theological writers in modern Church history. He wrote extensively on almost every aspect of our faith together with engaging prose. And yet, so little is known about his remarkable teachings. Fortunately, through Mr. Marr's book we now have greater access to Newman's works as he has expertly selected many relevant portions from them, guiding us through the many challenges we all face today. Surely an assortment of the best of our beloved Cardinal."

— Deacon Jack Sullivan, Pembroke, Massachusetts,
recipient of Newman's first miracle leading to his beatification

"Dr. Marr's engagement with Newman in this collection of writings is both scholarly and deeply personal. The volume draws together the saint's incisive intellect and pastoral sensitivities unlike any other that I have encountered. One would be hard-pressed to find a better introduction to Newman's spirit in so few pages."

— C. Michael Shea, author of *Newman's Early Roman Catholic Legacy, 1845–1854.*

"God has given us John Henry Newman for precisely these times in the Church. Every Catholic will find in his writings a remedy for many of the ills that beset us. This book offers us a wonderful place to begin a journey with Newman. In it, you will encounter the straightforward clarity of a shepherd and the fiery love of a saint."

— Meghan Cokeley, Director of the Office for the New Evangelization, Archdiocese of Philadelphia

"This book exudes the spirit of Saint Newman, which Marr expounds so thoroughly and insightfully in the introduction. It pleads with the reader, not merely to ponder, but to act in light of what the saint proclaims. The field of Newman studies is so often lost in insular plodding. This book mines the core of Newman's urgent appeal to the reader's inmost self—through its lean, incisive selections, heart truly calls to heart!"

— Bo Bonner, Director of Mission, Mercy College of Health Sciences

*Ex Libris*

# John Henry Newman

Compiled by Ryan Marr

*Pauline*
BOOKS & MEDIA

Library of Congress Control Number: 2019943678
CIP data is available.

ISBN-10: 0-8198-4038-6
ISBN-13: 978-0-8198-4038-7

The Scripture quotations contained herein are directly quoted from works written by John Henry Newman.

Excerpts from papal and magisterium texts copyright © Libreria Editrice Vaticana. All rights reserved. Used with permission.

Some alterations have been made to the punctuation that Newman used so as to bring the text into closer conformity with contemporary rules of grammar. None of these changes affects the meaning of the quotations.

Cover design by Rosana Usselmann

Cover photo: © National Portrait Gallery, London

Published by Pauline Books & Media, 50 Saint Pauls Avenue, Boston, MA 02130-3491

Printed in the U.S.A.

www.pauline.org

Pauline Books & Media is the publishing house of the Daughters of St. Paul, an international congregation of women religious serving the Church with the communications media.

1 2 3 4 5 6 7 8 9                    23 22 21 20 19

*To Dr. Kenneth Parker,*
*who has taught me most of what I know about Newman,*
*and whose scholarship in service to the Church*
*is an example to many.*

# Contents

### ❧—∞ THE INCARNATE WORD ∞—❧

### ❧—∞ OUR LADY ∞—❧

#### ❧∞ A GOOD DEATH ∞❧

#### ❧∞ HOLDING FAST TO THE TRUTH ∞❧

# Introduction

When John Henry Newman (1801–1890) was made a cardinal of the Roman Catholic Church in 1879, he took as his motto the phrase *Cor ad cor loquitur*—which translated means, "Heart speaks to heart." As someone who has spent many hours poring over Newman's writings, this phrase has always meant a great deal to me. I've been reading Newman for over a decade now, but my fascination with his work has never been a matter of merely historical interest. Newman's voice, as many recognized during his lifetime, was destined to endure long after his death. As with the works of other saintly theologians, there is something perpetually alive, and life-giving, about the essays and sermons that Newman left us. In this respect, I concur with Muriel Spark who once remarked that, "[Newman] is far less dead, to me, than many of my contemporaries."[1] Among the many friends in my life, Newman is near the top of the list in terms of having shaped the way that I view God, and it was largely through his influence that I was led into the Catholic Church.

I first encountered Newman's work while wrapping up graduate studies at Duke Divinity School, where I was preparing to become a Protestant minister. During my final semester at Duke, I was doing some side-reading as a break from my normal course of studies, when an article by Rusty Reno in the journal *First Things* ("Out of the Ruins") inspired me to look more closely at Newman's conversion from Anglicanism to Roman Catholicism. What I found in Newman's writings did in fact speak to my heart and, frankly, shook me to the core. While Newman could be incredibly nuanced in his treatment of a given theological topic, he also had a profound gift for cutting right to the heart of a matter. Imagine being on the verge of entering Protestant ministry and reading Newman's blunt observation that, "To be deep in history is to cease to be a Protestant."[2] Needless to say, upon reading this I had to investigate the claim for myself. I knew that I could not remain a dispassionate handler of Newman's theological heritage; this was a writer who demanded a response from his readers.

Newman's writings possess this quality, I believe, because of the way that he understood his vocation as a theologian. There is a venerable Christian maxim that says, "The theologian is one who prays. And if you pray truly, you will be a theologian." Unfortunately, in our own day, there are far too many academic theologians who are indifferent to this idea and who go about teaching theology without necessarily being grounded in a life of prayer. This kind of approach would have been completely foreign to Newman. One of his personal mottos was, "Life is for action,"[3] and on more than one occasion he warned others that there was a real danger in being inspired by an idea or work of art but then failing to translate that inspiration into action. As applied to theology, this statement reminds us that the study of God can never be a merely intellectual endeavor. Prayer, as Newman recognized, is the lifeblood of authentic theology. To study the truths of the faith without regularly turning to prayer is not only empty but perilous. "Our God is a consuming fire"[4] and has to be approached with due reverence if we are to avoid idolatrous understandings of the Divine.

Newman's conviction about the nature of the theological vocation—that it must be rooted in prayer and oriented to action/conversion—had a noticeable impact on how he went about composing his own books. His *Essay on the Development of Doctrine*, for instance, is a carefully crafted, thickly woven essay—and can prove difficult for beginning students to work through—but in no way did Newman intend the piece as an abstract intellectual exercise. Addressing his readers directly in the conclusion to that essay, Newman reminds them, "Time is short, eternity is long." In light of this fact, they should be careful not to dismiss what they have read as a "mere matter of present controversy" nor to delay a decision by wrapping themselves "round in the associations of years past."[5] The first several chapters in the essay lay out abundant evidence in support of the Roman Communion's claim to be the one, holy, catholic, and apostolic Church. This is either true or it's not. If true, Newman insists, it demands conversion on the part of those who remain outside her fold.

As I slowly worked my way through his various writings, I came to believe that Newman was right on this point and, therefore, that I must cease to be Protestant. This emerging conviction came as news to my wife, Rachel, who for some time had been preparing for life as a pastor's spouse, which in some Protestant circles can take on a vocational shape of its own. Outside of that specific issue, the prospect of entering the Catholic Church was intimidating for both of us for several reasons. High on the list was the disappointment that such a decision would bring to relatives and friends. A number of our closest loved ones were—and remain—committed Evangelical Protestants. Some of them harbor deep-seated suspicion of all things Roman Catholic, and at the time we wondered what becoming Catholic might mean for these relationships—including with our parents. Not surprisingly, there were career concerns as well. Entering the Catholic fold would significantly limit the kinds of ministry opportunities available to me, and Rachel justifiably wondered what the purpose of seven years of theological education had been if I was going to have to pursue a totally unrelated career path.

To be honest, at the time I didn't have good answers to those concerns, and for a while things became even more difficult. Rachel took instruction in the faith with me during the 2006–2007 academic year, but as Easter approached she decided that she could not in good conscience enter the Catholic Church. So for a few years (she became Catholic in 2010), there was a division within our marriage at the level of our most deeply held convictions. In this area of my life as well, though, Newman's voice lifted my spirit during difficult times. As is the case with most of us, Newman had to pass through various trials and tribulations during his adult life, but through it all he demonstrated remarkable trust in God. Whenever I felt discouraged, then, I turned to Newman's example for consolation. One prayer that became particularly meaningful for me was a brief reflection that Newman composed about God having a plan for his life:

> God has created me to do Him some definite service. He has committed some work to me which He has not committed to another. I have my mission—I never may know it in this life, but I shall be told it in the next . . . I am a link in a chain, a bond of connection between persons. He has not created me for naught. I shall do good; I shall do His

work . . . [God] does nothing in vain . . . He knows what
He is about. He may take away my friends. He may throw
me among strangers. He may make me feel desolate, make
my spirits sink, hide my future from me—still He knows
what He is about.[6]

Newman wrote this prayer in his own search for comfort
amid desolation, but it displays an enduring relevance and
startling universality. Suffering, disappointment, and grief
eventually find all of us, but they do not have to be the final
word on our lives. The one source of hope that will never fail
us is the Creator and Lord of the universe. Newman knew
this truth experientially. When he wrote about God's sus-
taining love for him, the words flowed from his heart and
into the hearts of others. They still do to this day.

———— ❦ ————

Newman's voice from the grave echoes loudly in our era,
in which the default position for most is skepticism rather
than belief and where the relentless pursuit of wealth and
pleasure has usurped the longing for eternal realities. In our
day, we could use more preachers like Newman. While he
never lost sight of God's abundant mercies, he was also
unafraid to challenge the unrepentant and refused to miti-
gate the harsh demands of the Gospel for the sake of social
approval or out of a fear not to offend. In his preaching,
Newman consistently brought conversations about the

Christian life back to the urgency of holiness. "Be you content," he wrote, "with nothing short of perfection."[7] Aiming lower than perfection, in his view, does not demonstrate humility but is quite simply settling for less than what God has intended for us. Our lives now, Newman wrote elsewhere, should look like the great saints whom we read about in the pages of the New Testament. As those who "dwell in the full light of the Gospel," he said, and who have access to "the full grace of the Sacraments . . . there is no reason except our own willful corruption" that we are not already "walking in the steps of [the Apostles]."[8]

It is passages like this one that continue to call me back to repentance. One thing I greatly admire in Newman is his impatience for half measures. From his perspective, God is not asking us to tweak our behavior here and there but to be totally transformed into the image of Christ. When we resist the movement of God's grace, we are living contrary to our own nature because Christ shows us what it means to be truly human. Sometimes what holds us back, though, are not dramatic sins but spiritual apathy—an embarrassing tendency to give up at the first sign of difficulty. For myself, I long for God's peace but recoil from the burning flame of his love when it shines a light on an area of my life where I still insist that "my will be done." Or, even more damning perhaps, I'm simply too lazy to cooperate with the grace that is being extended to me. To read Newman's reflections on the gravity of sin, and to take them seriously, is a potent antidote to any lingering temptation to downplay what is at stake in the call to obedience.

In appealing to Newman in this manner, I do not mean to suggest that his life had no rough edges, or that he somehow transcended all personality conflicts. Anyone who has read Newman's personal correspondence knows that he could be curt with interlocutors, and in his famous quarrels with other Catholic leaders (e.g., with William George Ward and Cardinal Manning) blame arguably fell as much on Newman as it did on his opponents. These facets of Newman's life shouldn't overly disturb us though. Theologically speaking, Catholics confess that the Blessed Virgin Mary was kept free from the stain of original sin, and tradition holds that John the Baptist was sanctified while still in the womb. All the rest of us, Newman included, stumble toward perfection. But Newman's extraordinary sanctity was no less remarkable for not being immediate, and because we have such an extensive written record of those times that Newman struggled with doubt and failure, he represents a saint that many modern persons can look to as a reminder that God has a plan for our lives no matter what struggles are presently weighing us down.

To put the matter somewhat colloquially, Newman was a very human saint. When one reads his letters and diaries, there is no mistaking that in Newman we have a fully flesh and blood human person, someone who faced all of the attendant struggles that normally confront an individual on the path toward holiness. Against the backdrop of Newman's meticulous journaling of his spiritual journey, God's grace stands out all the more. In light of the work that God accomplished in and through Newman—even, or perhaps especially, when things looked particularly bleak in his life— those of us with a devotion to this saint are able to find encouragement to persevere in the face of our own difficulties.

Regardless of where you are in the journey of life, Newman's voice has the potential to speak grace and truth into your experience. One theme that recurs throughout his writings is the importance of developing an abiding trust in God's loving providence. So often, like Peter on the Sea of Galilee, we feel overwhelmed by the storms raging around us. Newman recognized this kind of fear as one of the most common factors that knocked Christians off the right path, so he returned again and again both in his preaching and in his personal correspondence to the core issue of trust in God. Whenever I feel alone or anxious, I take solace in the words of Newman, knowing that they flowed out of a profound experience of God's care amid troubles that at times must have seemed insurmountable. Like Newman, I'm comforted by the reminder that "God has created me to do Him some definite service"—that He "has committed some work to me which He has not committed to another."[9] My hope for you as you pick up this volume is that, through familiarizing yourself with Newman's words, you too can come to know the same confidence that he had in God's loving care, so that together we might pray: "May [God] support us all the day long, till the shades lengthen, and the evening comes, and the busy world is hushed, and the fever of life is over, and our work is done! Then in His mercy may He give us safe lodging, and a holy rest, and peace at the last!"[10]

⸻ ❧ ⸻

Newman's life spanned nearly the entire nineteenth century, and it's amazing to consider just how much changed for him between the circumstances of his youth and his final years as a Catholic priest and theologian. Newman was raised in a conventional Anglican home, and later in life he described the nature of his religious upbringing as one centered on Bible reading. As a child Newman knew well the content of his faith, but these beliefs did not become real for him until a conversion experience at the age of fifteen. Newman described the transformation in his outlook this way: "When I was fifteen (in the autumn of 1816), a great change of thought took place in me. I fell under the influences of a definite Creed, and received into my intellect impressions of dogma, which, through God's mercy, have never been effaced or obscured."[11] For the next half-decade or so, Newman lived his Christianity in the manner of a devout evangelical, but over time he adopted the stance of a high church Anglican. He began studies at Trinity College, Oxford, in 1817, taking his degree there three years later. In April of 1822 he was awarded a fellowship at Oriel College, another college within the University of Oxford, which eventually became the epicenter of Tractarianism, also known as the Oxford Movement. Through a series of pamphlets, or *Tracts for the Times*, Newman and a circle of likeminded intellectuals sought to return the Church of England to its Catholic roots.

Newman served as the *de facto* leader of the Oxford Movement from 1833—the year that John Keble gave his sermon on "National Apostasy"—until 1841, when Newman published Tract 90, which argued that the Thirty-Nine Articles of the Church of England could be interpreted in line with official Roman Catholic doctrine. Although Newman anticipated that some members of his communion would find this claim troubling, he was not prepared for what happened next. Harsh criticism rained down upon Newman's Tract, not only from the heads of colleges at Oxford, who thought that he had betrayed the mission of their university, but also from two dozen bishops—including his own ordinary, who sternly ordered him to desist from publishing any further tracts. In the wake of this controversy, Newman stepped away from his responsibilities at Oxford and withdrew to a quasi-monastic arrangement at Littlemore, where his newfound doubts regarding the apostolicity of Anglicanism continued to grow. A few years later, on October 9, 1845, Newman was officially received into the Catholic Church by an Italian Passionist priest by the name of Dominic Barberi (who was beatified by Pope Paul VI in 1963).[12]

Newman's four-and-a-half decades as a Roman Catholic were marked by great personal trials but also by significant milestones, including several notable publications (e.g., his *Apologia*, *The Grammar of Assent*, and *A Letter to the Duke of Norfolk*, among others). Newman occasionally aroused suspicion on the part of ecclesiastical authorities, as for instance when he published an essay arguing that in deliberations on doctrinal questions the pastors of the Church should take the time to consult the lay faithful. Some ultramontane Catholics—that is, those who placed a strong emphasis on the authority of the pope—were particularly wary of Newman, for they worried that in becoming Catholic he had not become "Roman enough," believing that he harbored notions of church governance and the role of the faithful that were still essentially Protestant. Newman's reputation was eventually vindicated, however, not only in his lifetime when Pope Leo XIII made him a cardinal, but also in the following century, when his viewpoints on doctrinal development, the sense of the faithful, and papal infallibility were officially affirmed at the Second Vatican Council. Throughout the various twists and turns of his life as a Catholic, Newman remained firmly committed to the communion that he had joined himself to, and he compassionately counseled others not to allow scandals or abuses of power to weaken their sense that God was ultimately in charge and would preserve the Church from ever falling into error. Newman died from pneumonia on August 11, 1890. Per his request, he was laid to rest in the same burial plot as his good friend and fellow Oratorian, Ambrose St. John. On his memorial stone was engraved a Latin phrase, *Ex umbris et imaginibus in veritatem*—"Out of shadows and illusions into truth."

Newman's life story as presented above highlights mostly his intellectual accomplishments and experience of church affairs. But these elements of his life do not capture the full scope of Newman's significance. He was also a man of deep personal piety, with an impressive prayer life, and from all accounts a very holy priest. In an address from 1963, Pope Paul VI gave a particularly memorable encapsulation of Newman's courage, describing him as someone who "guided solely by love of the truth and fidelity to Christ, traced an itinerary, the most toilsome, but also the greatest, the most meaningful, the most conclusive, that human thought ever travelled during the [nineteenth] century, indeed one might say during the modern era, to arrive at the fullness of wisdom and of peace."[13] If I could leave you with a lasting impression to take away from learning about Newman's life, it would be what Paul VI talks about here. Supported by divine grace, may we, like Newman, seek the truth no matter the cost, so that one day we might arrive at the fullness of wisdom and of peace—blessed to hear the words that we trust have already been spoken over Newman: "Well done, thou good and faithful servant. Enter thou into the joy of thy Lord."[14]

## *Note from the Compiler*

One final word: Newman's Victorian rhetoric can sometimes sound foreign to our ears, and the density of his prose means that it can prove difficult to wade through.[15] Nevertheless, persevere dear reader! I firmly believe that any effort you put forth to understand and internalize Newman's insights will be abundantly rewarded. The path ahead is strenuous, but the end result for your spiritual life will be great indeed.

# FAITH

*True faith teaches us to do numberless disagreeable things for Christ's sake, to bear petty annoyances, which we find written down in no book. In most books Christian conduct is made grand, elevated, and splendid, so that any one, who only knows of true religion from books, and not from actual endeavours to be religious, is sure to be offended at religion when he actually comes upon it, from the roughness and humbleness of his duties, and his necessary deficiencies in doing them. It is beautiful in a picture to wash the disciples' feet; but the sands of the real desert have no lustre in them to compensate for the servile nature of the occupation.*

*Parochial and Plain Sermons,*
Vol. 2, Sermon 30, 374

# 1

# Faith, a Gift of God

Faith is the gift of God, and not a mere act of our own, which we are free to exert when we will. It is quite distinct from an exercise of reason, though it follows upon it. I may feel the force of the argument for the Divine origin of the Church; I may see that I ought to believe; and yet I may be unable to believe. This is no imaginary case; there is many a man who has ground enough to believe, who wishes to believe, but who cannot believe. It is always indeed his own fault, for God gives grace to all who ask for it, and use it, but still such is the fact that conviction is not faith. Take the parallel case of obedience; many a man knows he ought to obey God, and does not and cannot—through his own fault, indeed, but still he cannot; for through grace only can he obey. Now, faith is not a mere conviction in reason; it is a firm assent, it is a clear certainty greater than any other certainty; and this is wrought in the mind by the grace of God, and by it alone.

*Discourses Addressed to Mixed Congregations*, 224

# 2

# The Church, the Oracle of God

No one can be a Catholic without a simple faith, that what the Church declares in God's name is God's word, and therefore true. A man must simply believe that the Church is the oracle of God; he must be as certain of her mission as he is of the mission of the Apostles. Now, would any one ever call him certain that the Apostles came from God, if, after professing his certainty, he added, that perhaps he might have reason to doubt one day about their mission? Such an anticipation would be a real, though latent, doubt, betraying that he was not certain of it at present. A person who says, "I believe just at this moment, but perhaps I am excited without knowing it, and I cannot answer for myself, that I shall believe tomorrow," does not believe now. A man who says, "Perhaps I am in a kind of delusion, which will one day pass away from me, and leave me as I was before"; or "I believe as far as I can tell, but there may be arguments in the background which will change my view," such a man has not faith at all . . . [T]o make provision for future doubt is to doubt at present. It proves I am not in a fit state to become a Catholic now. I may love by halves, I may obey by halves; I cannot believe by halves: either I have faith, or I have it not.

*Discourses Addressed to Mixed Congregations*, 215–217

# 3

# Assent

Now, in the first place, what is faith? it is assenting to a doctrine as true, which we do not see, which we cannot prove, because God says it is true, who cannot lie. And further than this, since God says it is true, not with His own voice, but by the voice of His messengers, it is assenting to what man says, not simply viewed as a man, but to what he is commissioned to declare as a messenger, prophet, or ambassador from God.

*Discourses Addressed to Mixed Congregations*, 194–195

# 4

# Looking to God,
# Our Source of Comfort

We are in the dark about ourselves. When we act, we are groping in the dark, and may meet with a fall any moment ... The management of our hearts is quite above us. Under these circumstances it becomes our comfort to look up to God. "Thou, God, seest me!" Such was the consolation of the forlorn Hagar in the wilderness. He knoweth whereof we are made, and He alone can uphold us. He sees with most appalling distinctness all our sins, all the windings and recesses of evil within us; yet it is our only comfort to know this and to trust Him for help against ourselves. To those who have a right notion of their weakness, the thought of their Almighty Sanctifier and Guide is continually present.

They believe in the necessity of a spiritual influence to change and strengthen them, not as a mere abstract doctrine, but as a practical and most consolatory truth, daily to be fulfilled in their warfare with sin and Satan.

*Parochial and Plain Sermons,* Vol. 1, 173–174

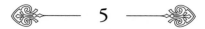

# 5

# **Faith in Action**

I t is not an easy thing to learn that new language which Christ has brought us. He has interpreted all things for us in a new way; He has brought us a religion which sheds a new light on all that happens. Try to learn this language. Do not get it by rote, or speak it as a thing of course. Try to understand what you say. Time is short, eternity is long; God is great, man is weak; he stands between heaven and hell; Christ is his Saviour; Christ has suffered for him. The Holy Ghost sanctifies him; repentance purifies him, faith justifies, works save. These are solemn truths, which need not be actually spoken, except in the way of creed or of teaching, but which must be laid up in the heart. That a thing is true is no reason that it should be said but that it should be done, that it should be acted upon, that it should be made our own inwardly.

*Parochial and Plain Sermons*, Vol. 5, 44–45

# HOLINESS

*[E]ven supposing a man of unholy life were suffered to enter heaven, he would not be happy there, so that it would be no mercy to permit him to enter . . . Nay, I will venture to say more than this—it is fearful, but it is right to say it—that if we wished to imagine a punishment for an unholy, reprobate soul, we perhaps could not fancy a greater than to summon it to heaven. Heaven would be hell to an irreligious man.*

Parochial and Plain Sermons,
Vol. 1, Sermon 1, 3 and 7

# 6

# Grace

There is no truth, my brethren, which Holy Church is more earnest in impressing upon us than that our salvation from first to last is the gift of God. It is true indeed that we merit eternal life by our works of obedience; but that those works are meritorious of such a reward, this takes place, not from their intrinsic worth, but from the free appointment and bountiful promise of God; and that we are able to do them at all is the simple result of His grace. That we are justified is of His grace; that we have the dispositions for justification is of His grace; that we are able to do good works when justified is of His grace; and that we persevere in those good works is of His grace. Not only do we actually depend on His power from first to last, but our destinies depend on His sovereign pleasure and inscrutable counsel. He holds the arbitration of our future in His hands; without an act of His will, independent of ours, we should not have been brought into the grace of the Catholic Church; and without a further act of His will, though we are now members of it, we shall not be brought on to the glory of the kingdom of Heaven. Though a soul justified can merit eternal life, yet neither can it merit to be justified nor can it merit to remain justified to the end; not only is a state of grace the condition and the life of all merit, but grace brings us into that state of grace, and grace continues us in it; and thus, as I began by saying, our salvation from first to last is the gift of God.

*Discourses Addressed to Mixed Congregations*, 124–125

# 7

# A Religion of Practice, Not Sentiment

Beware lest your religion be one of sentiment merely, not of practice. Men may speak in a high imaginative way of the ancient Saints and the Holy Apostolic Church, without making the fervour or refinement of their devotion bear upon their conduct. Many a man likes to be religious in graceful language; he loves religious tales and hymns, yet is never the better Christian for all this. The works of every day, these are the tests of our glorious contemplations, whether or not they shall be available to our salvation; and he who does one deed of obedience for Christ's sake, let him have no imagination and no fine feeling, is a better man and returns to his home justified rather than the most eloquent speaker and the most sensitive hearer of the glory of the Gospel, if such men do not practice up to their knowledge.

*Parochial and Plain Sermons,*
Vol. 1, Sermon 20, 269–270

# 8

# Prompt Obedience

This, then, is the lesson taught us by St. Paul's conversion: promptly to obey the call. If we do obey it, to God be the glory, for He it is who works in us. If we do not obey, to ourselves be all the shame, for sin and unbelief work in us. Such being the state of the case, let us take care to act accordingly—being exceedingly alarmed lest we should *not* obey God's voice when He calls us, yet not taking praise or credit to ourselves if we do obey it. This has been the temper of all saints from the beginning—working out their salvation with fear and trembling, yet ascribing the work to Him who wrought in them to will and do of His good pleasure; obeying the call, and giving thanks to Him who calls, to Him who fulfils in them their calling . . .

Such are the instances of Divine calls in Scripture, and their characteristic is this: to require instant obedience, and next to call us we know not to what, to call us on in the darkness. Faith alone can obey them.

*Parochial and Plain Sermons*,
Vol. 8, Sermon 2, 19 and 22

## 9

# The Warfare Between the Church and the World

Behold here the true origin and fountain-head of the warfare between the Church and the world; here they join issue and diverge from each other. The Church is built upon the doctrine that impurity is hateful to God, and that concupiscence is its root; with the Prince of the Apostles, her visible Head, she denounces "the corruption of concupiscence which is in the world,"[16] or that corruption in the world which comes of concupiscence; whereas the corrupt world defends, nay, I may even say, sanctifies that very concupiscence which is the world's corruption. Just as its bolder teachers, as you know, my brethren, hold that the laws of this physical creation are so supreme, as to allow of their utterly disbelieving in the existence of miracles, so, in like manner, it deifies and worships human nature and its impulses, and denies the power and the grant of grace. This is the source of the hatred which the world bears to the Church; it finds a whole catalogue of sins brought into light and denounced, which it would fain believe to be no sins at all; it finds itself, to its indignation and impatience, surrounded with sin, morning, noon, and night; it finds that a stern law lies against it in matters where it believed it was its own master and need not think of God; it finds guilt accumulating upon it hourly, which nothing can prevent, nothing remove, but a higher power, the grace of God. It finds itself in danger of being humbled to the earth as a rebel, instead of being allowed to indulge its self-dependence and self-complacency. Hence it takes its stand on nature, and denies or rejects divine grace. Like the proud spirit in the beginning, it wishes to find its supreme good in its own self, and nothing above it; it undertakes to be sufficient for its own happiness; it has no desire for the supernatural, and therefore does not believe in it. And because nature cannot rise above nature, it will not believe that the narrow way is possible; it hates those who enter upon it as if pretenders and hypocrites, or laughs at their aspirations as romance and fanaticism, lest it should have to believe in the existence of grace.

*Discourses Addressed to Mixed Congregations*, 149–151

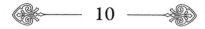

# 10

# The Value of One Single Soul

The Church aims, not at making a show, but at doing a
work. She regards this world, and all that is in it, as a
mere shadow, as dust and ashes, compared with the value of
one single soul. She holds that, unless she can, in her own
way, do good to souls, it is no use her doing anything; she
holds that it were better for sun and moon to drop from
heaven, for the earth to fail, and for all the many millions
who are upon it to die of starvation in extremest agony, so far
as temporal affliction goes, than that one soul, I will not say
should be lost, but should commit one single venial sin,
should tell one wilful untruth, though it harmed no one, or
steal one poor farthing without excuse. She considers the
action of this world and the action of the soul simply

incommensurate, viewed in their respective spheres; she would rather save the soul of one single wild bandit . . . or [one lowly] beggar . . . than draw a hundred lines of railroad through the length and breadth of Italy, or carry out a sanitary reform, in its fullest details, in [numerous cities], except so far as these great [civic] works tended to some spiritual good beyond them.

*Certain Difficulties Felt by Anglicans
in Catholic Teaching*, Vol. 1, 239–240

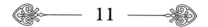

## 11

# Sin, the Mortal Enemy of the All-Holy

Sin is an easy thing to us; we think little of it; we do not understand how the Creator can think much of it; we cannot bring our imagination to believe that it deserves retribution, and when even in this world punishments follow upon it, we explain them away or turn our minds from them. But consider what sin is in itself; it is rebellion against God; it is a traitor's act who aims at the overthrow and death of His sovereign; it is that, if I may use a strong expression, which, could the Divine Governor of the world cease to be, would be sufficient to bring it about. Sin is the mortal enemy of the All-holy, so that He and it cannot be together . . .

*Discourses Addressed to Mixed Congregations*, 335

# 12

# Conversion

The heart is commonly reached, not through the reason, but through the imagination, by means of direct impressions, by the testimony of facts and events, by history, by description. Persons influence us, voices melt us, looks subdue us, deeds inflame us. Many a man will live and die upon a dogma; no man will be a martyr for a conclusion.

*An Essay in Aid of a Grammar of Assent*, 92–93

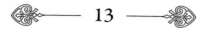

# 13

# Prayer

P rayer is to spiritual life what the beating of the pulse and the drawing of the breath are to the life of the body.

*Parochial and Plain Sermons,*
Vol. 7, Sermon 15, 209

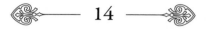

# 14

# Regularity in Prayer

He who gives up regularity in prayer has lost a principal means of reminding himself that spiritual life is obedience to a Lawgiver, not a mere feeling or a taste. Hence it is that so many persons, especially in the polished ranks of society, who are out of the way of temptation to gross vice, fall away into a mere luxurious self-indulgent devotion, which they take for religion; they reject every thing which implies self-denial, and regular prayer especially. Hence it is that others run into all kinds of enthusiastic fancies; because by giving up set private prayer in written forms, they have lost the chief rule of their hearts . . . And others, who are exposed to the seductions of sin, altogether fall away from the same omission. Be sure, my brethren, whoever of you is persuaded to disuse his morning and evening prayers, is giving up the armour which is to secure him against the wiles of the Devil.

*Parochial and Plain Sermons*, Vol. 1, Sermon 19, 253

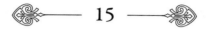

# 15

# Fix Your Hearts on Higher Things

Do not indulge visions of earthly good, fix your hearts on higher things, let your morning and evening thoughts be points of rest for your mind's eye, and let those thoughts be upon the narrow way and the blessedness of heaven and the glory and power of Christ your Saviour. Thus will you be kept from unseemly risings and fallings, and steadied in an equable way. Men in general will know nothing of this; they witness not your private prayers, and they will confuse you with the multitude they fall in with. But your friends and acquaintance will gain a light and a comfort from your example; they will see your good works and be led to trace them to their true secret source—the influences of the Holy Ghost sought and obtained by prayer. Thus they will glorify your heavenly Father, and in imitation of you will seek Him; and He who seeth in secret shall at length reward you openly.

*Parochial and Plain Sermons*, Vol. 1, Sermon 19, 256

# THE INCARNATE WORD

*[W]hen we confess God as Omnipotent only, we have gained but a half-knowledge of Him; His is an Omnipotence which can at the same time swathe Itself in infirmity and can become the captive of Its own creatures. He has, if I may so speak, the incomprehensible power of even making Himself weak. We must know Him by His names Emmanuel and Jesus to know Him perfectly.*

*Sermons Preached on Various Occasions, 87–88*

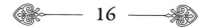

# 16

# The Ancient of Days

The Eternal Word, the Only-begotten Son of the Father, put off His glory, and came down upon earth, to raise us to heaven. Though He was God, He became man; though He was Lord of all, He became as a servant; "though He was rich, yet for our sakes He became poor, that we, through His poverty, might be rich."[17] He came from heaven in so humble an exterior that the self-satisfied Pharisees despised Him and treated Him as a madman or an impostor. When He spoke of His father Abraham and implied His knowledge of him, who was in truth but the creature of His hands, they said in derision, "Thou art not yet fifty years old, and hast Thou seen Abraham?" He made answer, "Amen, amen, I say unto you, Before Abraham was made, I am."[18] He had seen Abraham, who lived two thousand years before; yet in truth He was not two thousand years old, more than He was fifty. He was not two thousand years old, because He had no years; He was the Ancient of Days who never had beginning, and who never will have an end; who is above and beyond time; who is ever young and ever is beginning, yet never has not been and is as old as He is young; and was as old and as young when Abraham lived as when He came on earth in our flesh to atone for our sins . . . My brethren, if we could get ourselves to enter into this high and sacred thought, if we really contemplated the Almighty in Himself, then we should understand better what His incarnation is to us, and what it is in Him. I do not mean, if we worthily contemplated Him as He is; but, even if we contemplated Him in such a way as is really possible to us, if we did but fix our thoughts on Him, and make use of the reason which He has given us, we should understand enough of His greatness to feel the awfulness of His voluntary self-abasement.

*Discourses Addressed to Mixed Congregations*, 284–285

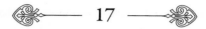

# 17

# Fully Human, Fully Divine

When the Eternal Word decreed to come on earth, He did not purpose, He did not work, by halves; but He came to be a man like any of us, to take a human soul and body, and to make them His own. He did not come in a mere apparent or accidental form, as Angels appear to men; nor did He merely over-shadow an existing man, as He overshadows His saints, and call Him by the name of God; but He "was made flesh."[19] He attached to Himself a manhood and became as really and truly man as He was God, so that henceforth He was both God and man, or, in other words, He was One Person in two natures, divine and human. This is a mystery so marvelous, so difficult, that faith alone firmly receives it; the natural man may receive it for a while, may think he receives it, but never really receives it; begins, as soon as he has professed it, secretly to rebel against it, evades it, or revolts from it. This he has done from the first; even in the lifetime of the beloved disciple men arose who said that our Lord had no body at all, or a body framed in the heavens, or that He did not suffer, but another suffered in His stead, or that He was but for a time possessed of the human form which was born and which suffered, coming into it at its baptism, and leaving it before its crucifixion, or, again, that He was a mere man. That "in the beginning was the Word, and the Word was with God, and the Word was God, and the Word was made flesh and dwelt among us,"[20] was too hard a thing for the unregenerate reason.

*Discourses Addressed to Mixed Congregations*, 344–345

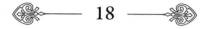

## 18

# A Willing Victim

Recollect that our Blessed Lord was in this respect different from us: that, though He was perfect man, yet there was a power in Him greater than His soul, which ruled His soul, for He was God. The soul of other men is subjected to its own wishes, feelings, impulses, passions, perturbations; His soul was subjected simply to His Eternal and Divine Personality. Nothing happened to His soul by chance, or on a sudden; He never was taken by surprise; nothing affected Him without His willing beforehand that it should affect Him. Never did He sorrow, or fear, or desire, or rejoice in spirit, but He first willed to be sorrowful, or afraid, or desirous, or joyful. When we suffer, it is because outward agents and the uncontrollable emotions of our minds bring suffering upon us. We are brought under the discipline of pain involuntarily, we suffer from it more or less acutely according to accidental circumstances, we find our patience more or less tried by it according to our state of mind, and we do our best to provide alleviations or remedies of it. We cannot anticipate beforehand how much of it will come upon us, or how far we shall be able to sustain it; nor can we say afterwards why we have felt just what we have felt, or why we did not bear the suffering better. It was otherwise with our Lord. His Divine Person was not subject, could not be exposed, to the influence of His own human affections and feelings, except so far as He chose. I repeat, when He chose to fear, He feared; when He chose to be angry, He was angry; when He chose to grieve, He was grieved. He was not open to emotion, but He opened upon Himself voluntarily the impulse by which He was moved. Consequently, when He determined to suffer the pain of His vicarious passion, whatever He did, He did, as the Wise Man says, *instanter*, "earnestly," with His might; He did not do it by halves; He did not turn away His mind from the suffering as we do— (how should He, who came to suffer, who could not have suffered but of His own act?) no, He did not say and unsay, do and undo; He said and He did; He said, "Lo, I come to do Thy will, O God; sacrifice and offering Thou wouldest not, but a body hast Thou fitted to Me."[21] He took a body in order that He might suffer; He became man, that He might suffer as man; and when His hour was come, that hour of Satan and of darkness, the hour when sin was to pour its full malignity upon Him, it followed that He offered Himself wholly, a holocaust, a whole burnt-offering—as the whole of His body, stretched out upon the Cross, so the whole of His soul, His whole advertence, His whole consciousness, a mind awake, a sense acute, a living cooperation, a present, absolute intention, not a virtual permission, not a heartless submission: this did He present to His tormentors. His passion was an action; He lived most energetically while He lay languishing, fainting, and dying. Nor did He die, except by an act of the will; for He bowed His head, in command as well as in resignation, and said, "Father, into Thy hands I commend My Spirit;"[22] He gave the word, He surrendered His soul, He did not lose it.

*Discourses Addressed to Mixed Congregations*, 329–331

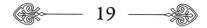

# 19

# Because He First Loved Us

So is it, O dear and gracious Lord, "the day of death is better than the day of birth, and better is the house of mourning than the house of feasting."[23] Better for me that Thou shouldst come thus abject and dishonourable, than hadst Thou put on a body fair as Adam's when he came out of Thy Hand. Thy glory sullied, Thy beauty marred, those five wounds welling out blood, those temples torn and raw, that broken heart, that crushed and livid frame: they teach me more than wert Thou Solomon "in the diadem wherewith his mother crowned him in the day of his heart's joy." The gentle and tender expression of that Countenance is no new beauty or created grace; it is but the manifestation, in a human form, of Attributes which have been from everlasting. Thou canst not change, O Jesus; and, as Thou art still Mystery, so wast Thou always Love. I cannot comprehend Thee more than I did before I saw Thee on the Cross; but I have gained my lesson. I have before me the proof that in spite of Thy awful nature, and the clouds and darkness which surround it, Thou canst think of me with a personal affection. Thou hast died that I might live. "Let us love God," says Thy Apostle, "because He first hath loved us."[24] I can love Thee now from first to last, though from first to last I cannot understand Thee. As I adore Thee, O Lover of souls, in Thy humiliation, so will I admire Thee and embrace Thee in Thy infinite and everlasting power.

*Discourses Addressed to Mixed Congregations*, 303–304

## 20

# The Voluntary Suffering of Our Lord

You see then, my brethren, how voluntary was the mission and death of our Lord; if an instance can be imagined of voluntary suffering, it is this. He came to die when He need not have died; He died to satisfy for what might have been pardoned without satisfaction; He paid a price which need not have been asked, nay, which needed to be accepted when paid. It may be said with truth, that, rigorously speaking, one being can never, by his own suffering, simply discharge the debt of another's sin. Accordingly, He died, not in order to exert a peremptory claim on the Divine justice, if I may so speak—as if He were bargaining in the market-place, or pursuing a plea in a court of law—but in a more loving, generous, munificent way, did He shed that blood, which was worth ten thousand lives of men, worth more than the blood of all the sons of Adam poured out together, in accordance with His Father's will, who, for wise reasons unrevealed, exacted it as the condition of their pardon.

*Discourses Addressed to Mixed Congregations*, 306–307

# OUR LADY

*If we have faith to admit the Incarnation itself, we must admit it in its fulness; why then should we start at the gracious appointments which arise out of it, or are necessary to it, or are included in it? If the Creator comes on earth in the form of a servant and a creature, why may not His Mother, on the other hand, rise to be the Queen of heaven, and be clothed with the sun, and have the moon under her feet?*

*Discourses Addressed to Mixed Congregations, 355*

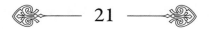

# 21

# Mary, Our Pattern of Faith

Little is told us in Scripture concerning the Blessed Virgin, but there is one grace of which the Evangelists make her the pattern, in a few simple sentences—of Faith. Zacharias questioned the Angel's message, but "Mary said, Behold the handmaid of the Lord; be it unto me according to thy word."[25] Accordingly Elisabeth, speaking with an apparent allusion to the contrast thus exhibited between her own highly-favoured husband, righteous Zacharias, and the still more highly-favoured Mary, said, on receiving her salutation, "Blessed art thou among women, and blessed is the fruit of thy womb; Blessed is she that believed, for there shall be a performance of those things which were told her from the Lord."[26]

But Mary's faith did not end in a mere acquiescence in Divine providences and revelations: as the text informs us, she "pondered" them. When the shepherds came and told of the vision of Angels, which they had seen at the time of the Nativity, and how one of them announced that the Infant in her arms was "the Saviour, which is Christ the Lord,"[27] while others did but wonder, "Mary kept all these things, and pondered them in her heart."[28] Again, when her Son and Saviour had come to the age of twelve years and had left her for awhile for His Father's service and had been found, to her surprise, in the Temple, amid the doctors, both hearing them and asking them questions, and had, on her addressing Him, vouchsafed to justify His conduct, we are told, "His mother kept all these sayings in her heart."[29] And accordingly, at the marriage-feast in Cana, her faith anticipated His first miracle, and she said to the servants, "Whatsoever He saith unto you, do it."[30]

Thus St. Mary is our pattern of Faith, both in the reception and in the study of Divine Truth. She does not think it enough to accept, she dwells upon it; not enough to possess, she uses it; not enough to assent, she developes it; not enough to submit the Reason, she reasons upon it; not indeed reasoning first and believing afterwards, with Zacharias, yet first believing without reasoning, next from love and reverence, reasoning after believing. And thus she symbolizes to us not only the faith of the unlearned, but of the doctors of the

Church also, who have to investigate, and weigh, and define, as well as to profess the Gospel; to draw the line between truth and heresy; to anticipate or remedy the various aberrations of wrong reason; to combat pride and recklessness with their own arms; and thus to triumph over the sophist and the innovator.

*Oxford University Sermons*, Sermon 15, 312–314

# 22

# A Daughter of Eve Unfallen

Suppose Eve had stood the trial and not lost her first grace; and suppose she had eventually had children; those children from the first moment of their existence would, through divine bounty, have received the same privilege that she had ever had; that is, as she was taken from Adam's side, in a garment, so to say, of grace, so they in turn would have received what may be called an immaculate conception. They would have then been conceived in grace, as in fact they are conceived in sin. What is there difficult in this doctrine? What is there unnatural? Mary may be called, as it were, a daughter of Eve unfallen. You believe with us that St. John Baptist had grace given to him three months before his birth, at the time that the Blessed Virgin visited his mother.

He accordingly was not immaculately conceived, because he was alive before grace came to him; but our Lady's case only differs from his in this respect: that to her the grace of God came, not three months merely before her birth, but from the first moment of her being, as it had been given to Eve.

*Certain Difficulties Felt by Anglicans*
*in Catholic Teaching*, Vol. 2, 47

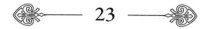 23

# The Immaculate Conception

But it may be said, How does this enable us to say that [Mary] was conceived without *original sin*? If Anglicans knew what we mean by original sin, they would not ask the question. Our doctrine of original sin is not the same as the Protestant doctrine. "Original sin," with us, cannot be called sin, in the mere ordinary sense of the word "sin;" it is a term denoting Adam's sin as transferred to us, or the state to which Adam's sin reduces his children; but by Protestants it seems to be understood as sin in much the same sense as actual sin. We, with the Fathers, think of it as something negative, Protestants as something positive.[31] Protestants hold that it is a disease, a radical change of nature, an active poison internally corrupting the soul, infecting its primary elements, and disorganizing it; and they fancy that we ascribe a different nature from ours to the Blessed Virgin, different from that of her parents and from that of fallen Adam. We hold nothing of the kind; we consider that in Adam she died, as others; that she was included, together with the whole race, in Adam's sentence; that she incurred his debt, as we do; but that, for the sake of Him who was to redeem her and us upon the Cross, to her the debt was remitted by anticipation; on her the sentence was not carried out, except indeed as regards her natural death, for she died when her time came, as others. All this we teach, but we deny that she had original sin; for by original sin we mean, as I have already said, something negative, [namely], this only: the *deprivation* of that supernatural unmerited grace which Adam and Eve had on their first formation—deprivation and the consequences of deprivation. Mary could not merit, any more than they, the restoration of that grace; but it was restored to her by God's free bounty, from the very first moment of her existence, and thereby, in fact, she never came under the original curse, which consisted in the loss of it. And she had this special privilege in order to fit her to become the Mother of her and our Redeemer, to fit her mentally, spiritually for it, so that, by the aid of the first grace, she might so grow in grace, that, when the Angel came and her Lord was at hand, she might be "full of grace,"[32] prepared as far as a creature could be prepared, to receive Him into her bosom.

*Certain Difficulties Felt by Anglicans
in Catholic Teaching*, Vol. 2, 48–49

# 24

# Clothed with the Sun,
# Crowned with the Stars

Coming back then to the Apocalyptic vision [of Revelation 12],[33] I ask, If the Woman ought to be some real person, who can it be whom the Apostle saw and intends and delineates, but that same Great Mother to whom the chapters in the Proverbs are accommodated? And let it be observed, moreover, that in this passage, from the allusion made in it to the history of the fall, Mary may be said still to be represented under the character of the Second Eve. I make a farther remark: it is sometimes asked, Why do not the sacred writers mention our Lady's greatness? I answer, she was, or may have been, alive when the Apostles and

Evangelists wrote—there was just one book of Scripture certainly written after her death, and that book does (so to say) canonize and crown her.

But if all this be so, if it is really the Blessed Virgin whom Scripture represents as clothed with the sun, crowned with the stars of heaven, and with the moon as her footstool, what height of glory may we not attribute to her?[34] and what are we to say of those who, through ignorance, run counter to the voice of Scripture, to the testimony of the Fathers, to the traditions of East and West, and speak and act contemptuously towards her whom her Lord delighteth to honour?

*Certain Difficulties Felt by Anglicans*
*in Catholic Teaching*, Vol. 2, 60–61

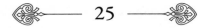

# 25

# Exalted for the Sake of Her Son

[Mary's relationship to her Son highlights] the harmonious consistency of the revealed system, and the bearing of one doctrine upon another; Mary is exalted for the sake of Jesus. It was fitting that she, as being a creature, though the first of creatures, should have an office of ministration [that is, the role of intercessor and mediatrix of graces]. She, as others, came into the world to do a work, she had a mission to fulfil; her grace and her glory are not for her own sake, but for her Maker's; and to her is committed the custody of the Incarnation: this is her appointed office—"A Virgin shall conceive, and bear a Son, and they shall call His Name Emmanuel."[35] As she was once on earth and was personally the guardian of her Divine Child, as she carried Him in her womb, folded Him in her embrace, and suckled Him at her breast, so now, and to the latest hour of the Church, do her glories and the devotion paid her proclaim and define the right faith concerning Him as God and man. Every church which is dedicated to her, every altar which is raised under her invocation, every image which represents her, every litany in her praise, every Hail Mary for her continual memory, does but remind us that there was One who, though He was all-blessed from all eternity, yet for the sake of sinners, "did not shrink from the Virgin's womb."[36] Thus she is the *Turris Davidica*, as the Church calls her, "the Tower of David,"[37] the high and strong defence of the King of the true Israel; and hence the Church also addresses her in the Antiphon, as having "alone destroyed all heresies in the whole world."[38]

*Discourses Addressed to Mixed Congregations*, 348–349

# 26

# Guardian of Orthodoxy

And the confession that Mary is *Deipara*, or the Mother of God, is that safeguard wherewith we seal up and secure the doctrine of the [Incarnation] from all evasion, and that test whereby we detect all the pretences of those bad spirits of "Antichrist which have gone out into the world"[39] ... And here, my brethren, a fresh thought opens upon us, which is naturally implied in what has been said. If the *Deipara* is to witness of Emmanuel, she must be necessarily more than the *Deipara*. For consider: a defence must be strong in order to be a defence; a tower must be, like that Tower of David, "built with bulwarks;" "a thousand bucklers hang upon it, all the armour of valiant men."[40] It would not have sufficed, in order to bring out and impress on us the idea that God is man, had His Mother been an ordinary person. A mother without a home in the Church, without dignity, without gifts, would have been, as far as the defence of the Incarnation goes, no mother at all. She would not have remained in the memory or the imagination of men. If she is to witness and remind the world that God became man, she must be on a high and eminent station for the purpose. She must be made to fill the mind, in order to suggest the lesson. When she once attracts our attention, then, and not till then, she begins to preach Jesus. "Why should she have such prerogatives," we ask, "unless He be God? and what must He be by nature, when she is so high by grace?" This is why she has other prerogatives besides, namely, the gifts of personal purity and intercessory power, distinct from her maternity; she is personally endowed that she may perform her office well; she is exalted in herself that she may minister to Christ.

*Discourses Addressed to Mixed Congregations*, 347 and 349–350

# 27

# On the Fitness
# of the Glories of Mary

And now, my dear brethren, what is befitting in us, if all that I have been telling you is befitting in Mary? If the Mother of Emmanuel ought to be the first of creatures in sanctity and in beauty; if it became her to be free from all sin from the very first, and from the moment she received her first grace to begin to merit more; and if such as was her beginning, such was her end, her conception immaculate and her death an assumption; if she died, but revived, and is exalted on high; what is befitting in the children of such a Mother, but an imitation, in their measure, of her devotion, her meekness, her simplicity, her modesty, and her sweetness? Her glories are not only for the sake of her Son, they are for our sakes also. Let us copy her faith, who received God's message by the angel without a doubt; her patience, who endured St. Joseph's surprise without a word; her obedience, who went up to Bethlehem in the winter and bore our Lord in a stable; her meditative spirit, who pondered in her heart what she saw and heard about Him; her fortitude, whose heart the sword went through; her self-surrender, who gave Him up during His ministry and consented to His death.

Above all, let us imitate her purity, who, rather than relinquish her virginity, was willing to lose Him for a Son. O my dear children, young men and young women, what need have you of the intercession of the Virgin-mother, of her help, of her pattern, in this respect! What shall bring you forward in the narrow way, if you live in the world, but the thought and patronage of Mary? What shall seal your senses, what shall tranquilize your heart, when sights and sounds of danger are around you, but Mary? What shall give you patience and endurance, when you are wearied out with the length of the conflict with evil, with the unceasing necessity of precautions, with the irksomeness of observing them, with the tediousness of their repetition, with the strain upon your mind, with your forlorn and cheerless condition, but a loving communion with her! She will comfort you in your discouragements, solace you in your fatigues, raise you after your falls, reward you for your successes. She will show you her Son, your God and your all.

*Discourses Addressed to Mixed Congregations*, 374–375

## 28

# Intercessor for the Church Militant

[ A ]s the Gospel shows, [our Lord] on various occasions [allowed] those who were near Him to be the channels of introducing supplicants to Him or of gaining miracles from Him, as in the instance of the miracle of the loaves; and if on one occasion He seems to repel His Mother when she told Him that wine was wanting for the guests at the marriage feast, it is obvious to remark on it, that, by saying that she was then separated from Him ("What have I to do with thee?")[41] *because* His hour was not yet come, He implied, that when that hour was come, such separation would be at an end. Moreover, in fact He did at her intercession work the miracle to which her words pointed.

I consider it impossible then, for those who believe the Church to be one vast body in heaven and on earth, in which every holy creature of God has his place, and of which prayer is the life, when once they recognize the sanctity and dignity of the Blessed Virgin, not to perceive immediately that her office above is one of perpetual intercession for the faithful militant, and that our very relation to her must be that of clients to a patron, and that, in the eternal enmity which exists between the woman and the serpent, while the serpent's strength lies in being the Tempter, the weapon of the Second Eve and Mother of God is prayer.

*Certain Difficulties Felt by Anglicans*
*in Catholic Teaching*, Vol. 2, 72–73

## 29

# Our Lady of Sorrows

And further still, interest your dear Mother, the Mother of God, in your success; pray to her earnestly for it; she can do more for you than any one else. Pray her by the pain she suffered when the sharp sword went through her, pray her by her own perseverance, which was in her the gift of the same God of whom you ask it for yourselves. God will not refuse you, He will not refuse her, if you have recourse to her succour. It will be a blessed thing in your last hour, when flesh and heart are failing, in the midst of the pain, the weariness, the restlessness, the prostration of strength, and the exhaustion of spirits, which then will be your portion, it will be blessed indeed to have her at your side, more tender than an earthly mother, to nurse you and to whisper peace. It will be most blessed, when the evil one is making his last effort, when he is coming on you in his might to pluck you away from your Father's hand, if he can—it will be blessed indeed if Jesus, if Mary and Joseph are then with you, waiting to shield you from his assaults and to receive your soul. If they are there, all are there: Angels are there, Saints are there, heaven is there, heaven is begun in you, and the devil has no part in you. That dread day may be sooner or later, you may be taken away young, you may live to fourscore, you may die in your bed, you may die in the open field, but if Mary intercedes for you, that day will find you watching and ready. All things will be fixed to secure your salvation; all dangers will be foreseen, all obstacles removed, all aids provided. The hour will come, and in a moment you will be translated beyond fear and risk, you will be translated into a new state where sin is not, nor ignorance of the future, but perfect faith and serene joy, and assurance and love everlasting.

*Discourses Addressed to Mixed Congregations*, 143–144

# A GOOD DEATH

*Oh, my Lord and Saviour, support me in that hour
in the strong arms of Thy Sacraments and by the fresh
fragrance of Thy consolations. Let the absolving words
be said over me, and the holy oil sign and seal me,
and Thy own Body be my food, and Thy Blood my
sprinkling; and let my sweet Mother, Mary, breathe
on me, and my Angel whisper peace to me, and my
glorious Saints . . . smile upon me; that in them all,
and through them all, I may receive the gift of perseverance, and die as I desire to live: in Thy faith, in Thy
Church, in Thy service, and in Thy love. Amen.*

*Meditations and Devotions*, 290

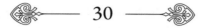

# 30

# Christ's Presence with Us at Death

Let us take to ourselves these comfortable thoughts, both in the contemplation of our own death, or upon the death of our friends. Wherever faith in Christ is, there is Christ Himself. He said to Martha, "Believest thou this?" Wherever there is a heart to answer, "Lord, I believe," there Christ is present.[42] There our Lord vouchsafes to stand, though unseen—whether over the bed of death or over the grave; whether we ourselves are sinking or those who are dear to us. Blessed be his name! nothing can rob us of this consolation: we will be as certain, through His grace, that He is standing over us in love, as though we saw Him. We will not, after our experience of Lazarus's history, doubt an instant that He is thoughtful about us. He knows the beginnings of our illness, though He keeps at a distance. He knows when to remain away and when to draw near. He notes down the advances of it, and the stages. He tells truly when His friend Lazarus is sick and when he sleeps. We all have experience of this in the narrative before us, and henceforth, so be it! will never complain at the course of His providence. Only, we will beg of Him an increase of faith—a more lively perception of the curse under which the world lies, and of our own personal demerits, a more understanding view of the mystery of His Cross, a more devout and implicit reliance on the virtue of it, and a more confident persuasion that He will never put upon us more than we can bear, never afflict His brethren with any woe except for their own highest benefit.

*Parochial and Plain Sermons*, Vol. 3, Sermon 10, 138

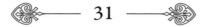

## 31

# Illuminating Grace

Faith and prayer alone will endure in that last dark hour, when Satan urges all his powers and resources against the sinking soul. What will it avail us then, to have devised some subtle argument, or to have led some brilliant attack, or to have mapped out the field of history, or to have numbered and sorted the weapons of controversy, and to have the homage of friends and the respect of the world for our successes—what will it avail to have had a position, to have followed out a work, to have re-animated an idea, to have made a cause to triumph, if after all we have not the light of faith to guide us on from this world to the next? Oh, how fain shall we be in that day to exchange our place with the humblest and dullest and most ignorant of the sons of men, rather than to stand before the judgment-seat in the lot of him who has received great gifts from God, and used them for self and for man, who has shut his eyes, who has trifled with truth, who has repressed his misgivings, who has been led on by God's grace, but stopped short of its scope, who has neared the land of promise, yet not gone forward to take possession of it!

*Discourses Addressed to Mixed Congregations*, 190–191

— 32 —

# One Glance of Thee Sufficeth

How different is the feeling with which the loving soul, on its separation from the body, approaches the judgment-seat of its Redeemer! It knows how great a debt of punishment remains upon it, though it has for many years been reconciled to Him; it knows that purgatory lies before it, and that the best it can reasonably hope for is to be sent there. But to see His face, though for a moment! to hear His voice, to hear Him speak, though it be to punish! O Saviour of men, it says, I come to Thee, though it be in order to be at once remanded from Thee; I come to Thee who art my Life and my All; I come to Thee on the thought of whom I have lived all my life long. To Thee I gave myself when first I had to take a part in the world; I sought Thee for my chief good early, for early didst Thou teach me, that good elsewhere there was none. Whom have I in heaven but Thee? whom have I desired on earth, whom have I had on earth, but Thee? whom shall I have amid the sharp flame but Thee? Yea, though I be now descending thither, into "a land desert, pathless and without water,"[43] I will fear no ill, for Thou art with me. I have seen Thee this day face to face, and it sufficeth; I have seen Thee, and that glance of Thine is sufficient for a century of sorrow, in the nether prison. I will live on that look of Thine, though I see Thee not, till I see Thee again, never to part from Thee.

*Discourses Addressed to Mixed Congregations*, 81–82

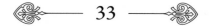

33

# The Thought of God, the Stay of the Soul

Life passes, riches fly away, popularity is fickle, the senses decay, the world changes, friends die. One alone is constant; One alone is true to us; One alone can be true; One alone can be all things to us; One alone can supply our needs; One alone can train us up to our full perfection; One alone can give a meaning to our complex and intricate nature; One alone can give us tune and harmony; One alone can form and possess us. Are we allowed to put ourselves under His guidance? this surely is the only question. Has He really made us His children and taken possession of us by His Holy Spirit? Are we still in His kingdom of grace, in spite of our sins? The question is not whether we should go, but whether

He will receive. And we trust that, in spite of our sins, He will receive us still, every one of us, if we seek His face in love unfeigned and holy fear. Let us then do our part, as He has done His, and much more. Let us say with the Psalmist, "Whom have I in heaven but Thee? and there is none upon earth I desire in comparison of Thee. My flesh and my heart faileth; but God is the strength of my heart, and my portion for ever."[44]

*Parochial and Plain Sermons*, Vol. 5, Sermon 22, 326

# HOLDING FAST TO THE TRUTH

*From the age of fifteen, dogma has been the fundamental principle of my religion: I know no other religion; I cannot enter into the idea of any other sort of religion; religion as a mere sentiment is to me a dream and a mockery. As well can there be filial love without the fact of a father, as devotion without the fact of a Supreme Being. What I held in 1816, I held in 1833, and I hold in 1864. Please God, I shall hold it to the end.*

*Apologia Pro Vita Sua, 49*

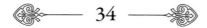

## 34

# On the Development of Doctrine

It is indeed sometimes said that the stream is clearest near the spring. Whatever use may fairly be made of this image, it does not apply to the history of a philosophy or belief, which on the contrary is more equable, and purer, and stronger, when its bed has become deep, and broad, and full. It necessarily rises out of an existing state of things, and for a time savours of the soil. Its vital element needs disengaging from what is foreign and temporary, and is employed in efforts after freedom which become more vigorous and hopeful as its years increase. Its beginnings are no measure of its capabilities, nor of its scope. At first no one knows what it is, or what it is worth. It remains perhaps for a time quiescent; it tries, as it were, its limbs, and proves the ground under it, and feels its way. From time to time it makes essays which fail, and are in consequence abandoned. It seems in suspense which way to go; it wavers, and at length strikes out in one definite direction. In time it enters upon strange territory; points of controversy alter their bearing; parties rise and fall around it; dangers and hopes appear in new relations; and old principles reappear under new forms. It changes with them in order to remain the same. In a higher world it is otherwise, but here below to live is to change, and to be perfect is to have changed often.

*An Essay on the Development of Christian Doctrine*, 40

## 35

# Resistance to the Spirit of Liberalism

In a long course of years I have made many mistakes. I have nothing of that high perfection which belongs to the writings of Saints, [namely], that error cannot be found in them; but what I trust that I may claim all through what I have written is this—an honest intention, an absence of private ends, a temper of obedience, a willingness to be corrected, a dread of error, a desire to serve Holy Church, and, through Divine mercy, a fair measure of success. And, I rejoice to say, to one great mischief I have from the first opposed myself. For thirty, forty, fifty years I have resisted to the best of my powers the spirit of liberalism in religion.

Never did Holy Church need champions against it more sorely than now, when, alas! it is an error overspreading, as a snare, the whole earth; and on this great occasion, when it is natural for one who is in my place to look out upon the world, and upon Holy Church as in it, and upon her future, it will not, I hope, be considered out of place, if I renew the protest against it which I have made so often.

Liberalism in religion is the doctrine that there is no positive truth in religion, but that one creed is as good as another; and this is the teaching which is gaining substance and force daily. It is inconsistent with any recognition of any religion, as *true*. It teaches that all are to be tolerated, for all are matters of opinion. Revealed religion is not a truth, but a sentiment and a taste; not an objective fact, not miraculous; and it is the right of each individual to make it say just what strikes his fancy. Devotion is not necessarily founded on faith. Men may go to Protestant Churches and to Catholic, may get good from both and belong to neither. They may fraternise together in spiritual thoughts and feelings, without having any views at all of doctrine in common, or seeing the need of them. Since, then, religion is so personal a peculiarity and so private a possession, we must of necessity ignore it in the intercourse of man with man. If a man puts on a new religion every morning, what is that to you? It is as impertinent to think about a man's religion as about his sources of income or his management of his family. Religion is in no sense the bond of society.

*Addresses to Cardinal Newman with His Replies,*
"Biglietto Speech," 63–65

## 36

# An Intelligent and Well-Instructed Laity

As troubles and trials circle round you, He will give you what you want at present—"a mouth, and wisdom, which all your adversaries shall not be able to resist and gainsay."[45] "There is a time for silence, and a time to speak;"[46] the time for speaking is come. What I desiderate in Catholics is the gift of bringing out what their religion is; it is one of those "better gifts," of which the Apostle bids you be "zealous."[47] You must not hide your talent in a napkin, or your light under a bushel. I want a laity not arrogant, not rash in speech, not disputatious, but men who know their religion, who enter into it, who know just where they stand, who know what they hold and what they do not, who know their creed so well that they can give an account of it, who know so much of history that they can defend it. I want an intelligent, well-instructed laity; I am not denying you are such already: but I mean to be severe, and, as some would say, exorbitant in my demands; I wish you to enlarge your knowledge, to cultivate your reason, to get an insight into the relation of truth to truth, to learn to view things as they are, to understand how faith and reason stand to each other, what are the bases and principles of Catholicism, and where lie the main inconsistences and absurdities of the Protestant theory. I have no apprehension you will be the worse Catholics for familiarity with these subjects, provided you cherish a vivid sense of God above, and keep in mind that you have souls to be judged and to be saved. In all times the laity have been the measure of the Catholic spirit; they saved the Irish Church three centuries ago, and they betrayed the Church in England. Our rulers were true, our people were cowards. You ought to be able to bring out what you feel and what you mean, as well as to feel and mean it; to expose to the comprehension of others the fictions and fallacies of your opponents; and to explain the charges brought against the Church, to the satisfaction, not, indeed, of bigots, but of men of sense, of whatever cast of opinion . . . Ignorance is the root of all littleness; he who can realise the law of moral conflicts, and the incoherence of falsehood, and the issue of perplexities, and the end of all things, and the Presence of the Judge, becomes, from the very necessity of the case, philosophical, long-suffering, and magnanimous.

*Lectures on the Present Position of Catholics in England,* 390–391

 — 37 —

# The Infidelity of the Future

A t all times the enemy of souls assaults with fury the Church which is their true Mother, and at least threatens and frightens when he fails in doing mischief. And all times have their special trials which others have not. And so far I will admit that there were certain specific dangers to Christians at certain other times, which do not exist in this time. Doubtless, but still admitting this, still I think that the trials which lie before us are such as would appall and make dizzy even such courageous hearts as St. Athanasius, St. Gregory I, or St. Gregory VII. And they would confess that dark as the prospect of their own day was to them severally, ours has a darkness different in kind from any that has been before it.

*Faith and Prejudice and Other Unpublished Sermons*, 116–117

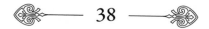

# 38

# The Passion and the Pride of Man

Quarry the granite rock with razors, or moor the vessel with a thread of silk; then may you hope with such keen and delicate instruments as human knowledge and human reason to contend against those giants, the passion and the pride of man.

*The Idea of a University*, 121

# 39

# Conscience

Certainly, if I am obliged to bring religion into after-dinner toasts, (which indeed does not seem quite the thing) I shall drink—to the Pope, if you please—still, to Conscience first, and to the Pope afterwards.

*Certain Difficulties Felt by Anglicans*
*in Catholic Teaching*, Vol. 2, 261

# 40

# Conscience, the Aboriginal Vicar of Christ

The rule and measure of duty is not utility, nor expedience, nor the happiness of the greatest number, nor State convenience, nor fitness, order, and the *pulchrum* [i.e., what is beautiful or noble]. Conscience is not a long-sighted selfishness, nor a desire to be consistent with oneself; but it is a messenger from Him, who, both in nature and in grace, speaks to us behind a veil, and teaches and rules us by His representatives. Conscience is the aboriginal Vicar of Christ,[48] a prophet in its informations, a monarch in its peremptoriness, a priest in its blessings and anathemas, and, even though the eternal priesthood throughout the Church could cease to be, in it the sacerdotal [or, priestly] principle would remain and would have a sway.

*Certain Difficulties Felt by Anglicans
in Catholic Teaching*, Vol. 2, 248–249

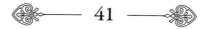

## 41

# Counterfeit Conscience

Conscience has rights because it has duties; but in this age, with a large portion of the public, it is the very right and freedom of conscience to dispense with conscience, to ignore a Lawgiver and Judge, to be independent of unseen obligations. It becomes a licence to take up any or no religion, to take up this or that and let it go again, to go to church, to go to chapel, to boast of being above all religions, and to be an impartial critic of each of them. Conscience is a stern monitor, but in this century it has been superseded by a counterfeit, which the eighteen centuries prior to it never heard of, and could not have mistaken for it, if they had. It is the right of self-will.

*Certain Difficulties Felt by Anglicans*
*in Catholic Teaching,* Vol. 2, 250

# TRUST IN DIVINE PROVIDENCE

*Lead, Kindly Light, amid the encircling gloom*
*Lead Thou me on!*
*The night is dark, and I am far from home—*
*Lead Thou me on!*
*Keep Thou my feet; I do not ask to see*
*The distant scene—one step enough for me.*

*Verses on Various Occasions*, 156

# 42

# A Link in a Chain

God has created me to do Him some definite service; He has committed some work to me which He has not committed to another. I have my mission—I never may know it in this life, but I shall be told it in the next. Somehow I am necessary for His purposes, as necessary in my place as an Archangel in his—if, indeed, I fail, He can raise another, as He could make the stones children of Abraham. Yet I have a part in this great work; I am a link in a chain, a bond of connexion between persons. He has not created me for naught. I shall do good, I shall do His work; I shall be an angel of peace, a preacher of truth in my own place, while not intending it, if I do but keep His commandments and serve Him in my calling.

Therefore I will trust Him. Whatever, wherever I am, I can never be thrown away. If I am in sickness, my sickness may serve Him; in perplexity, my perplexity may serve Him; if I am in sorrow, my sorrow may serve Him. My sickness, or perplexity, or sorrow may be necessary causes of some great end, which is quite beyond us. He does nothing in vain; He may prolong my life, He may shorten it; He knows what He is about. He may take away my friends, He may throw me among strangers, He may make me feel desolate, make my spirits sink, hide the future from me—still He knows what He is about.

O Adonai, O Ruler of Israel, Thou that guidest Joseph like a flock, O Emmanuel, O Sapientia, I give myself to Thee. I trust Thee wholly. Thou art wiser than I—more loving to me than I myself. Deign to fulfil Thy high purposes in me whatever they be—work in and through me. I am born to serve Thee, to be Thine, to be Thy instrument. Let me be Thy blind instrument. I ask not to see—I ask not to know—I ask simply to be used.

*Meditations and Devotions*, 301–302

## 43

# We Are Not Our Own

We are not our own, any more than what we possess is our own. We did not make ourselves; we cannot be supreme over ourselves. We cannot be our own masters. We are God's property by creation, by redemption, by regeneration. He has a triple claim upon us. Is it not our happiness thus to view the matter? Is it any happiness, or any comfort, to consider that we *are* our own? It may be thought so by the young and prosperous. These may think it a great thing to have everything, as they suppose, their own way—to depend on no one—to have to think of nothing out of sight—to be without the irksomeness of continual acknowledgment, continual prayer, continual reference of what they do to the will of another. But as time goes on, they, as all men, will find that

independence was not made for man—that it is an unnatural
state—may do for a while but will not carry us on safely to
the end. No, we are creatures; and, as being such, we have
two duties: to be resigned and to be thankful.

*Parochial and Plain Sermons*, Vol. 5, 83–84

# 44

# Christ the King

[M]en do not like to hear of the interposition of Providence in the affairs of the world; and they invidiously ascribe ability and skill to His agents, to escape the thought of an Infinite Wisdom and an Almighty Power. They will be unjust to their brethren, that they may not be just to Him; they will be wanton in their imputations, rather than humble themselves to a confession.

But for us, let us glory in what they disown; let us beg of our Divine Lord to take to Him His great power, and manifest Himself more and more, and reign both in our hearts and in the world. Let us beg of Him to stand by us in trouble, and guide us on our dangerous way. May He, as of old, choose "the foolish things of the world to confound the wise, and the weak things of the world to confound the things which are mighty"![49] May He support us all the day long, till the shades lengthen, and the evening comes, and the busy world is hushed, and the fever of life is over, and our work is done! Then in His mercy may He give us safe lodging, and a holy rest, and peace at the last!

*Sermons Bearing on Subjects of the Day*, 307

# 45

# He Calls Thee By Name

God beholds thee individually, whoever thou art. He "calls thee by thy name."[50] He sees thee, and understands thee, as He made thee. He knows what is in thee, all thy own peculiar feelings and thoughts, thy dispositions and likings, thy strength and thy weakness. He views thee in thy day of rejoicing, and thy day of sorrow. He sympathises in thy hopes and thy temptations. He interests Himself in all thy anxieties and remembrances, all the risings and fallings of thy spirit. He has numbered the very hairs of thy head and the cubits of thy stature. He compasses thee round and bears thee in his arms; He takes thee up and sets thee down. He notes thy very countenance, whether smiling or in tears, whether healthful or sickly. He looks tenderly upon thy hands and thy feet; He hears thy voice, the beating of thy heart, and thy very breathing. Thou dost not love thyself better than He loves thee. Thou canst not shrink from pain more than He dislikes thy bearing it; and if He puts it on thee, it is as thou would put it on thyself, if thou art wise, for a greater good afterwards. Thou art not only His creature (though for the very sparrows He has a care, and pitied the "much cattle" of Nineveh),[51] thou art man redeemed and sanctified, His adopted son, favoured with a portion of that glory and blessedness which flows from Him everlastingly unto the Only-begotten. Thou art chosen to be His, even above thy fellows who dwell in the East and South. Thou wast one of those for whom Christ offered up His last prayer, and sealed it with His precious blood. What a thought is this, a thought almost too great for our faith!

*Parochial and Plain Sermons*, Vol. 3, 124–125

# 46

# Not for Us to Know the Times and the Seasons

Providence always says, "*Stand still*, and see the salvation of God."[52] We must not dare to move, except He bids us. How different was the success of Moses afterwards, when God sent him! In like manner, the deliverers of Israel, in the period of the Judges, were, for the most part, expressly commissioned to their office. At another time, "the Lord delivered Sisera into the hand of a woman."[53] It is not for us "to know the times and the seasons which the Father hath put in His own power."[54]

*Discussions and Arguments*, 32–33

47

# Stand Still and See the Salvation of God

I lament it [the spread of apostasy in society] deeply, because I foresee that it may be the ruin of many souls; but I have no fear at all that it really can do aught of serious harm to the Word of God, to Holy Church, to our Almighty King, the Lion of the tribe of Judah, Faithful and True, or to His Vicar on earth. Christianity has been too often in what seemed deadly peril, that we should fear for it any new trial now. So far is certain; on the other hand, what is uncertain, and in these great contests commonly is uncertain, and what is commonly a great surprise when it is witnessed, is the particular mode by which, in the event, Providence rescues and saves His elect inheritance. Sometimes our enemy is turned into a friend; sometimes he is despoiled of that special virulence of evil which was so threatening; sometimes he falls to pieces of himself; sometimes he does just so much as is beneficial, and then is removed.

Commonly the Church has nothing more to do than to go on in her own proper duties, in confidence and peace; to stand still and to see the salvation of God.

*Addresses to Cardinal Newman with His Replies,*
"Biglietto Speech," 69–70

# Continuing in the School of John Henry Newman

As Newman would remind his listeners, "Life is for action!" There is a serious danger, he cautioned, in hearing or reading spiritual truths but then not acting upon them. Now that you have encountered some quotations drawn from his writings, how will you respond? As a starting point for applying Newman's insights, you may want to use the following study questions for meditation, journaling, group discussion, and prayer:

1. Newman describes right faith as an act of the intellect "done in a certain moral disposition." What connection do you see between one's conduct of life and coming to accept truths that have been revealed by God?

2. Does Newman's observation that "holiness [is] the result of many patient, repeated efforts after obedience" resonate with your own experience? What changes could you make to your daily schedule that would help you to develop habits of hearing and obeying God's voice?

3. Newman says that sin is "rebellion against God" and "the mortal enemy of the All-holy," yet that too often "we think little of it." In your own life, how might you be taking sin too lightly? How could you go about developing a proper sense of the gravity of your sins?

4. What steps are you taking today to prepare for a good death? Do you regularly ask God for the grace of final perseverance?

5. Based on what you've read from Newman, what would it look like to pattern your faith after Mary's and your life after Christ's?

6. What concrete steps could you take to practice abandonment to divine providence? Trusting that God has created you for some purpose, what is some definite service that you could undertake now? How do you plan to discern God's will moving forward?

# *Ex Libris*

John Henry Newman's literary output was astounding. His *Parochial and Plain Sermons*, which are just from the Anglican period of his life, comprise eight volumes of about 350 pages each, his *Letters and Diaries* some thirty-two volumes. Meanwhile, he produced around a dozen seminal essays that were more academic in nature. Consequently, it can be intimidating for the uninitiated to know where to begin in Newman's vast body of writings. The following overview is meant to orient the reader to some of Newman's key works and does not purport to be exhaustive.

## *Parochial and Plain Sermons*

This collection of Newman's Anglican sermons is a cornucopia of spiritual wisdom. Catholics who are unfamiliar with Newman's writings might at first worry how well

Newman's theology in these sermons squares with Catholic doctrine, but such a concern is unfounded. Newman was formed in the school of the fathers—that is, by reading the great writers of the first few centuries of Christian history—and on the basis of these sermons, it's clear that he thought very much like a Catholic long before becoming one. Individual sermons can be read in a single sitting and make for wonderful devotional reading.

## *An Essay on the Development of Christian Doctrine*

This is a more difficult work than the *Parochial and Plain Sermons*, but it rewards patient study. Newman composed the *Essay* while he was struggling with the decision about whether to enter the Catholic Church. The final product is Newman's demonstration of how Catholic teaching from later centuries represents an organic development of the apostolic deposit of faith, in much the same way that a mature oak tree is the full flowering of a tiny acorn. Once Newman felt that he had worked out this difficulty, he was convinced that it would be sinful to remain in his present state, and on October 9, 1845, he was received into the Roman Catholic Church by Dominic Barberi, an Italian Passionist priest.

## *The Idea of a University*

These lectures are a byproduct of Newman's time serving as the founding rector of the University of Ireland. Professionally, this was a trying experience for him, and he stepped down as rector disappointed with the overall direction of the project. Nevertheless, students of Newman remain grateful for this turn of events, as without his time in this role we would not have the *Idea of a University*, which is justifiably considered a classic in educational theory. Within the work Newman insists that a university, if it "professes to teach universal knowledge," must teach theology—as "theology is surely a branch of knowledge."[55] Theology, Newman goes on to say, is an antidote against "the perversion of other sciences,"[56] because it prevents them from assuming that they have a monopoly on all there is to know about reality. Overall, Newman's essay is a stirring manifesto for preserving the liberal arts that stands in stark contrast to the reductive and profit-driven approaches that drive so much of contemporary higher education.

## *Apologia pro Vita Sua*

Newman's *Apologia pro Vita Sua* (1864), or defense of his life, is one of the great spiritual autobiographies of the modern era, if not of all time. Newman was inspired to compose this "history of [his] spiritual opinions"[57] after Charles

Kingsley, a prominent novelist and university professor, accused him of lacking proper respect for the truth. The work quickly became a bestseller, and it was read eagerly by Anglicans as well as Catholics. When Newman first entered communion with Rome, some of his countrymen viewed the decision as a decidedly un-English thing to do. This book helped to restore Newman's reputation among many English Protestants, and in the decades afterward an increasing number of citizens came to see Newman as a shining light of the English intellectual heritage, even if his Catholic convictions made him stand out in the culture of his time.

## 1877 Preface to the Third Edition of the Via Media

The *via media* (or, "middle way") refers to a theory that Newman defended while he was still in the Church of England—namely, that Anglicanism cuts a middle path between the errors of Protestantism, on one side, and the errors of Roman Catholicism, on the other. Upon entering the Catholic Church, Newman of course abandoned this theory, but late in his life he chose to reissue some of his writings on the topic with a new preface and notes that were intended to clarify how a Catholic would approach issues raised in the text. Composed when he was in his mid-seventies, the 1877 Preface to volume one of the *Via Media* was one of the last major publications that Newman released.

In this brief, but substantive essay, Newman draws an analogy between the threefold office of Christ—as prophet, priest, and king—and "three essential powers or functions"[58] in the Church: namely, the Church's prophetical function, overseen by theologians; its priestly responsibilities, expressed in devotion; and its kingly or ruling power, centered in the hierarchy. Each office is necessary for the healthy functioning of the Church, but each is also prone to a particular weakness: theological reasoning tends towards rationalism, devotion can devolve into superstition, and power falls prey to ambition. Drawing upon these insights, Newman argued that corruption occurs when one of the offices oversteps its bounds and is not properly checked by the other two—for example, when the bishops, or rulers in the Church, make political expediency more important than fidelity to the ethical demands of the Gospel. Living as we are in a Church rocked by scandal, Newman's Preface is as timely today as it was when he first published it.

# Notes

1. Muriel Spark, "Foreword" to *Realizations: Newman's Selection of His* Parochial and Plain Sermons, ed. Vincent Ferrer Blehl (Collegeville, MN: Liturgical Press, 1964), ix.

2. John Henry Newman, *An Essay on the Development of Christian Doctrine* (London: B. M. Pickering, 1878), 8.

3. See, e.g., John Henry Newman, *Discussions and Arguments on Various Subjects* (London: B. M. Pickering, 1872), 295.

4. Hebrews 12:29.

5. Newman, *An Essay on the Development of Christian Doctrine*, 445.

6. John Henry Newman, *Meditations and Devotions of the Late Cardinal Newman*, ed. Rev. W. P. Neville (London: Longmans, Green, and Co., 1907), 301–302.

7. John Henry Newman, *Parochial and Plain Sermons*, vol. 1, no. 1 (London: Longmans, Green, and Co., 1907), 13.

8. Ibid., vol. 1, no. 6, 82. I am indebted to Ian Ker for drawing the connection between these insights from two of Newman's

sermons, "Holiness Necessary for Future Blessedness" and "The Spiritual Mind." For Fr. Ker's reflection on these sermons, see *The Achievement of John Henry Newman* (Notre Dame, IN: University of Notre Dame Press, 1990), 76–77.

9. Newman, *Meditations and Devotions*, 301.

10. John Henry Newman, *Sermons Bearing on Subjects of the Day* (London: Rivingtons, 1869), 307.

11. John Henry Newman, *Apologia pro Vita Sua* (London: Oxford University Press, 1913), 107.

12. As someone who went through the difficult experience of confessing all of the sins I committed between ages twelve and twenty-eight, I found some consolation in learning that Newman began his own first confession in the evening and then had to break for sleep before continuing the following morning with Father Barberi.

13. Pope Paul VI, *Acta Apostolicae Sedis*, annus 50, series 3, vol. 5 of *Commentarium Officiale* (Città del Vaticano: Typis Polyglottis Vaticanis, 1963), 1025. http://www.vatican.va/archive/aas/documents/AAS-55-1963-ocr.pdf

14. See Matthew 25:21.

15. If a specific quote proves particularly difficult to wrap your mind around, you may want to seek out its context. All of Newman's published writings are available at NewmanReader.org.

16. 2 Peter 1:4 (Douay-Rheims Version).

17. 2 Corinthians 8:9.

18. John 8:57–58.

19. John 1:14.

20. John 1:1 and 14.

21. Hebrews 10:5, quoting the Septuagint version of Psalm 40:6.

22. Luke 23:46.

23. Ecclesiastes 7:2.

24. 1 John 4:19.

25. Luke 1:38.

26. Luke 1:42 and 45.

27. Luke 2:11.

28. Luke 2:19.

29. Luke 2:51.

30. John 2:5.

31. In this sentence, Newman is using the terms "positive" and "negative" in a technical sense. He does not mean positive=good and negative=bad, as we normally use the terms today. Rather, Newman is saying that Catholics understand original sin as something *negative*, or lacking, in persons after the fall; whereas Protestants view it as a *positive* reality, that is, as something present and active. Because Protestants have a different understanding of what original sin entails, they sometimes misunderstand the teaching of the Immaculate Conception, assuming the doctrine to mean that Mary possessed a different nature from the rest of humanity. In actuality, however, Catholic teaching affirms the equality of Mary at the level of nature. The gift that was given to her was not a new nature, but restoration of the supernatural unmerited grace which our first parents had. As Newman affirms in this same excerpt, Mary did not merit her own salvation; rather, she was remitted the

debt of sin by anticipation. In other words, by the grace of God, Mary was kept free from the wound of original sin. The idea of a wound, or a deprivation, helps to frame what Newman means by use of the term "negative," as something that is lacking—not a "positive" reality, like a personal sin.

32. Luke 1:28.

33. Newman, here, is basing his theological reflection off the vision related by John the Seer in the twelfth chapter of Revelation. Within the context of that book, John has been granted mystical access to the temple in heaven. Upon approaching the holiest part of the temple, where the ark of the covenant is kept, he suddenly has a vision of "a woman clothed with the sun, with the moon under her feet, and on her head a crown of twelve stars" (Rev. 12:1). Since the early centuries of Christian history, biblical commentators have understood the woman in Revelation 12 to be a type both of Mary and of the Church. She gives birth to the Christ Child, or Messiah, and then is persecuted by Satan for her faithfulness. The original manuscripts, of course, would not have had chapter and verse numbers, so John's narration of these events would have moved directly from speaking about the inner sanctum of the temple to describing the woman clothed with the sun and wearing a diadem of twelve stars—that is, without a chapter break. Commentators have seen in this detail additional confirmation that Mary is the new (and greater) ark of the covenant, containing within herself the bread of life and possessing such purity that it was fitting for her to remain perpetually virgin.

34. See Revelation 12:1.

35. Matthew 1:23, based on the prophecy from Isaiah 7:14.

36. Quoting Saint Alphonsus Maria de' Liguori, *The Glories of Mary*, Part 2, Discourse 1 (New York: P. O'Shea, 1868), 269.

37. From the Litany of Loreto. Cf. Song of Songs 4:4.

38. From *The Little Office of the Blessed Virgin Mary*.

39. Cf. 1 John 4:1 and 3. Newman, in this excerpt, is making the argument that to affirm Mary as the Mother of God safeguards the doctrine of the Incarnation—i.e., that God himself, the Second Person of the Trinity, was made flesh and dwelt among us. According to the longstanding teaching of the Church, Jesus was fully divine and fully human from the moment of his conception. Some heretics were willing to call Mary the "Mother of the Messiah," but refused to use the title "Mother of God." As Newman points out, in refusing to affirm Mary's divine motherhood, they implicitly undermined the full divinity of the Incarnate Word.

40. Song of Songs 4:4.

41. John 2:4.

42. John 11:26–27.

43. Psalm 63:1.

44. Psalm 73:25–26.

45. Luke 21:15.

46. Ecclesiastes 3:7.

47. See 1 Corinthians 12:31.

48. By describing conscience as the "aboriginal Vicar of Christ," Newman is highlighting the fact that it is in and through our conscience, that we first hear the voice of God speaking to us. Conscience, Newman says elsewhere, has a twofold character:

when I act against my conscience, I not only have a cognitive sense that I have committed a wrong, but also feel an emotional response (shame), which testifies to the fact that I have offended *someone*. In this respect, conscience points beyond itself, both to the reality of a moral law *and* to the reality of a Lawgiver. Insofar as we listen to our conscience and seek to do what is right, we will be more properly disposed to receive God's Word, because when divine revelation reaches us, it will reinforce what we have already subtly perceived through our conscience.

49. 1 Corinthians 1:27.

50. Isaiah 43:1.

51. Cf. Matthew 10:29 and Jonah 4:11.

52. Exodus 14:13. Cf. Psalm 46:10.

53. Judges 4:9.

54. Acts 1:7.

55. John Henry Newman, *The Idea of a University Defined and Illustrated* (London: Longmans, Green, and Co., 1907), 20.

56. Ibid., 78.

57. John Henry Newman, *Apologia pro Vita Sua* (New York: Longmans, Green, and Co., 1908), v.

58. Avery Dulles, *John Henry Newman* (London: Continuum, 2009), 110.

# Bibliography

Dulles, Avery. *John Henry Newman*. London: Continuum, 2009.

Ker, Ian. *The Achievement of John Henry Newman*. Notre Dame, IN: University of Notre Dame Press, 1990.

Liguori, Alphonsus Maria de'. *The Glories of Mary*. New York: P. O'Shea, 1868.

Newman, John Henry. *Addresses to Cardinal Newman with His Replies*. London: Longmans, Green, and Co., 1905.

———. *Apologia pro Vita Sua*. New York: Longmans, Green, and Co., 1908.

———. *Certain Difficulties Felt by Anglicans in Catholic Teaching*. London: Longmans, Green, and Co., 1900.

———. *Discourses Addressed to Mixed Congregations*. London: Longmans, Green, and Co., 1906.

———. *Discussions and Arguments on Various Subjects*. London: B. M. Pickering, 1872.

———. *An Essay in Aid of a Grammar of Assent*. London: Longmans, Green, and Co., 1903.

———. *An Essay on the Development of Christian Doctrine*. London: Longmans, Green, and Co., 1909.

_____. *Faith and Prejudice and Other Unpublished Sermons*. New York: Sheed & Ward, 1956.

_____. *Fifteen Sermons Preached Before the University of Oxford, 1826–1843*. London: Longmans, Green, and Co., 1909.

_____. *The Idea of a University Defined and Illustrated*. London: Longmans, Green, and Co., 1907.

_____. *Lectures on the Present Position of Catholics in England*. London: Longmans, Green, and Co., 1908.

_____. *Meditations and Devotions of the Late Cardinal Newman*. Edited by Rev. W. P. Neville. London: Longmans, Green, and Co., 1907.

_____. *Parochial and Plain Sermons, in Eight Volumes*. London: Longmans, Green, and Co., 1907.

_____. *Sermons Bearing on Subjects of the Day*. London: Rivingtons, 1869.

_____. *Sermons Preached on Various Occasions*. London: Longmans, Green, and Co., 1908.

_____. *Verses on Various Occasions*. London: Longmans, Green, and Co., 1909.

Paul VI, Pope. *Acta Apostolicae Sedis*, annus 50, series 3, vol. 5 of *Commentarium Officiale*. Città del Vaticano: Typis Polyglottis Vaticanis, 1963. http://www.vatican.va/archive/aas/documents/AAS-55-1963-ocr.pdf

Spark, Muriel. "Foreword" to *Realizations: Newman's Selection of His* Parochial and Plain Sermons. Edited by Vincent Ferrer Blehl. Collegeville, MN: Liturgical Press, 1964.

# Other titles in the *Ex Libris* Series

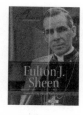

**Fulton J. Sheen**
*Compiled by Alexis Walkenstein*
0-8198-2747-9
$12.95

**G. K. Chesterton**
*Compiled by Dale Ahlquist*
0-8198-3153-0
$12.95

Coming soon!
**Edith Stein**

BOOKS & MEDIA

The Daughters of St. Paul operate book and media centers at the following addresses. Visit, call, or write the one nearest you today, or find us at www.paulinestore.org.

CALIFORNIA
3908 Sepulveda Blvd, Culver City, CA 90230          310-397-8676
3250 Middlefield Road, Menlo Park, CA 94025          650-562-7060

FLORIDA
145 S.W. 107th Avenue, Miami, FL 33174               305-559-6715

HAWAII
1143 Bishop Street, Honolulu, HI 96813               808-521-2731

ILLINOIS
172 North Michigan Avenue, Chicago, IL 60601         312-346-4228

LOUISIANA
4403 Veterans Memorial Blvd, Metairie, LA 70006      504-887-7631

MASSACHUSETTS
885 Providence Hwy, Dedham, MA 02026                 781-326-5385

MISSOURI
9804 Watson Road, St. Louis, MO 63126                314-965-3512

NEW YORK
115 E. 29th Street, New York City, NY 10016          212-754-1110

SOUTH CAROLINA
243 King Street, Charleston, SC 29401                843-577-0175

TEXAS
No book center; for parish exhibits or outreach evangelization, contact: 210-569-0500, or SanAntonio@paulinemedia.com, or P.O. Box 761416, San Antonio, TX 78245

VIRGINIA
1025 King Street, Alexandria, VA 22314               703-549-3806

CANADA
3022 Dufferin Street, Toronto, ON M6B 3T5            416-781-9131